Becoming an Insurance Professional

Jeff Davis

Introduction

Insurance is a very profitable and yet very hard business to succeed in. The majority of the positions are commissioned and the turn- over rate for new agents is probably second to no other industry.

Yet why do so many people engage on a career in Insurance? There are a lot of reasons a career in this field can be very rewarding; high income potential, renewals paid on people who keep the policies, promotions to management and overrides, etc. Many benefits are included in a sales career.

The pitfalls keep most agents from ever getting to the benefits. If you cannot survive in Insurance until things turn around for you, then you become a casualty.

This book has chapters addressing various areas of both gratitude and concern I found as an agent. I hope the insights will help you navigate through this career.

Jeff Davis

Insurance Sales Is a Business First

I have written articles in the past that have dealt with the selling of Insurance. What I want to do with this article is deal more with the business of Insurance.

Although most agents will start off as Independent Contractors they sometimes think of themselves as employees. They go to work a certain time each day, attend all the meetings, do what their manager expects and then look for a check by the end of the week. This mentality works well for the hourly employee but is the death of an Independent Contractor who is an Insurance Agent.

First, agents are only compensated for writing business that is issued and stays on the books. Period. There are some Insurance companies that will hire agents and give them a salary for a specific period of time but overall most agents work on straight commission. Understanding this means that each day an agent must ask themselves "is this activity going to help me write business?" If the answer is yes, great. If it is no, then you really need to minimize how much of it you do.

I remember working for a large Insurance carrier who required we come in twice a week to cold call. Plus on another day we had meetings that were supposedly motivational that could last well into the afternoon. You were still expected to produce. But after you have done this you realize that cold calling is one of the most ineffective ways to gain leads (takes a lot of time and typically you get few results). Add to that unpaid meetings that can take another day out of your week and you will have about 60% of your 5 day work week spent on activities that don't generate commissions.

Second, when you view your sales career as a business, expenses are very important to you. You have to pay to get a license, and then you pay to keep it through continuing ed classes and renewal fees. You must have a car to get to appointments and meetings and gas is very expensive. You have to have decent clothes to wear and you many need to invest in materials so that you can do your job (laptop, computer, and cell phone). Plus if you prospect you will need to pay for materials so that you can prospect such as leads (which are never free because you pay for them either directly or by accepting a smaller commission split from insurer) printing, copying materials, etc. Insurance is one business where your expenses can easily outpace your income.

The only way a business can exist is to create a profit (Commissions earned less expenses paid). This profit is what you and your family will live on. You must make sure you operate your business profitably so you can stay in business.

Look at how you run your sales career. Make it a profitable one!

Building Your Insurance Business

It is possible to build a profitable, sustainable Insurance business if you understand the components of building a good business.

Anyone who enters into the Insurance sales field should start off looking at this as a business. Anytime you work for someone and you are not receiving a guaranteed wage (such as working on a commission) you are in business for yourself. If you sell no policies, you get no commission which means no paycheck.

That being said let me offer you some principles on building a profitable insurance business;

1) Determine exactly what business you are in - What exactly do you do in Insurance sales? What is your product? Who is your client?

For example, if you sell Medicare Supplements, your clients will not be single 25 year olds. If you sell annuities your clients will not be college students.

Establish upfront that you are in the business of providing insurance policies to people who need and want them. The types of policies you sell may vary (life, health, annuities, auto, home, etc.) and no one is really successful trying to sell them all. You must determine what business you are in so that you can determine who your client should be. Don't market to the world; market to your niche!

2) Learn to work ON your business, not IN your business - many people in business fail because they focus too much time doing things in their business. Your job as an insurance agent is not to do everything but to make sure everything gets done. You have to look at your business from a global perspective. See what is and isn't working. What are you doing that is making you money and what is costing you?

3) Staff to your weaknesses - we all have weaknesses. Instead of spending a lot of time trying to strengthen your weaknesses, staff to them. Find out what you are not good at and then get other people who are good at that to do the work for you. Get administrative help if you are weak administratively. Have someone make your calls for you if you are not good on the phone. There are always people available who are strong in what you are weak at.

4) Focus on your strengths - every person who has ever done great things did it by focusing on their strengths. Larry Bird was a great basketball player known for hitting big shots. Every morning he shot 500 free throws to improve his accuracy. He was and still is one of the best big men to ever play the game known for his shooting prowess. Build your business on the things you are good at.

5) Delegate, delegate, delegate - Get help. Many companies you get contracted with will have administrative help. Use them. Hire outside contractors to help you build your business.

Your Career Success Is Up To You

Do you want a job or a career? When you have a job you get up and go to work, perform whatever duties are required of you and collect a paycheck. Many people who have jobs do so because they have to, not because they want to.

When you have a job that pays you enough to cover your bills it is very hard to quit it. Many times our jobs means we have a J.O.B. (just over broke) position and although we work 40 plus hours a week we never seem to get by. This makes us slaves to our positions and keeps us from looking to have something better. A job can keep you trapped in a position that is very hard to get away from.

A career is something else. It starts with knowing what you want to do each and every day. You prepare for what you will be doing each day by getting a good education. Then once you enter the field you want to work in you actually go to work each day enjoying what you do. You don't have a job: you have a hobby that you love doing and getting paid for each day.

I know this situation first hand. I have had more jobs than any of my friends. I would take a position, stay a few months and then move on because the jobs became boring; I wasn't making enough money, etc. I believed that the answer was in finding the right "job". What I found is when you pursue a career in an industry you want to be in, you can create the opportunity that will allow you to flourish at your work space.

Let me offer a few suggestions about pursuing a career;

1) **Be true to yourself** - know who you are, what you want and why you want it.

2) **Do what you love, the money will follow -** don't chase dollar bills. Refuse to work strictly for pay. Instead tap into your passion. Find out what you are willing to do for free and let money be the side benefit.

3) **Be honest** – crooks don't last in financial fields

People who have great careers tend to love what they do. When you are in that category you smile every day and become very grateful for the position you have.

I think finding what you love and then making it work for you is the best career choice anyone can make.

How to Build an Insurance Sales Career

It is important to think about what we will do as a career. Most of us will work at least 40 years doing something to generate money to support ourselves and our family. In addition people are living longer so you want to make sure that all those years working will allow you to put aside some assets to help you during retirement.

Insurance sales can be a great vehicle to do that. Here are some reasons why selling insurance may be right for you;

1) Helping people - a good agent leaves each satisfied client knowing he has helped them. Not only do you help families protect themselves against unexpected losses but you give them peace of mind.

2) Professional position - a career in Insurance sales means you have entered into a professional position. Not just anyone can do your job. You meet new and different people every day and the more you help people the more you establish yourself as a professional in this field.

3) A true sales position - all of the aspects of sales is covered in this position. You have to learn your product (training), you have to go and find clients who need your product (prospecting), you have to show them the benefit of getting your product today (presentation) and you have to be OK asking them for money (close).

4) Unlimited compensation - in most cases you will earn commission as a sales representative which means your income is only limited by how many policies you produce for the company. You can realistically earn a six figure income as a sale representative.

5) Management opportunities - for those who want to recruit and train others you can move into a management position and earn commissions from your sales team.

6) Time flexibility - most agents set their own schedules. You can arrange to be off any day of the week you choose and still earn what you need to for yourself and your family.

These are but a few of the benefits of a career in Insurance sales. You have to decide if being in sales is right for you. Not everyone can deal with the uncertainty of commissions, the constant "no thanks" you hear as people reject your presentation and he need to get up each day committed to being your best. But if you can do this, you will find this is a most lucrative and rewarding career choice.

Look into it. You may be pleasantly surprised.

Six Figure Income Is Possible

Have you ever wondered why some people consistently earn a six figure income while others struggle to make ends meet?

There is no real mystery to it at all. The answer is so simple it is easy to elude us. Let me give you the main reason why some earn six figures and others do not;

"Six figure income earners expect to earn at least that much. Those who fail to earn that don't expect to earn it anyway."

If you want to move into the category of one of those who earns a minimum six figures in personal income, let me offer some suggestions to point you in that path.

1) You must believe it is possible to earn six figures in Insurance sales - Salespeople have a habit of achieving incredible financial success. Your income is not limited. If you turn in 100 applications that become policies and your commission is $1000 per application, you just made six figures.

2) You must expect that if you do what is required, you too will earn six figures - there is a science to success. A positive mental attitude, an expectation of winning, believing in yourself and your personal worth are all characteristics you want to embrace. Success is able to be duplicated. Follow the path other successful agents have walked down and chances are you will experience the same results.

3) You must see yourself worthy of at least six figures - sadly, many people accept their lot in life as being a permanent one. It makes no difference where you have come from, what you did or didn't have what education you received, who your parents were etc. Yes, having support and advantages in life make succeeding easier but nothing is impossible to the person who thinks they can. Instead of looking at what you don't have, focus on what you do. Make your assets work for you.

4) You must plan to earn it - productive activity is the key to increased sales. How much is your average commission on a sale (not the company you work for average; what is your personal average)? How many presentations do you need in order to make a sale? How many calls must you make in order to do a presentation? What does it cost you to make a call (lead cost, gas to go prospecting, etc.)?

5) You must never, ever, ever quit - period. This is non-negotiable. You don't quit until you win. You plan and execute. You get knocked down and you get back up again. You focus on your goal, not your obstacle.

I ran track in high school. My coach told us "the one who wins a race is not the one concerned with the progress of his opponents. Every time you look at what another runner is doing you are taking away from your focus. Pay attention to your strides, your breathing and keep your eye on your goal. Nothing else matters."

Do you want to become someone who earns "six figures and beyond"? You can if you refuse to give up.

Go for it!!!

Sales Strategies for Insurance Agents

I believe that success leaves clues. People who start from nothing and build something great do so by employing strategies that gets them to their desired destination.

It begins in the mind. Whatever the mind can conceive and believe it can achieve. You must see yourself succeeding in sales, believe that it is possible to do so and then have corresponding actions that make what you believe a reality.

John Maxwell teaches on the laws of success. In one of his books he describes "the law of the lid." This law basically states that we all have self-imposed lids we put on ourselves that limits how far we can go in any chosen endeavor. We get to a certain point financially and then if it looks like we will go beyond that point we sabotage our future success. In essence, we hit our lid.

Let me give you an example. Maybe up unto this point you have only made $40,000 a year on your job. You decide to go all out in a sales career and suddenly you have the chance to earn $80,000. If $40,000 is the lid that you have subconsciously set for yourself you may find yourself doing things to prevent you from ever reaching $80,000. You may stop working. You may begin to slack off. Or you may get your manager and team so ticked off at you that you are fired.

We all have lids. We all have limitations we have placed on our lives. But it's only by trying do you ever discover what that lid is. Take a famous basketball player who comes from a modest family and then was drafted into the NBA and awarded a contract worth millions. Many such players not only earn the wealth but they refuse to squander it. There lid was a lot higher than their present circumstance at the time.

We can all raise the lid so that success will not scare you. Here are a few ways to do it.

A) Associate with people who have more than you do- when you get around successful people who have lots of what the world has to offer it can open your eyes to possibilities. One of my uncles has done real well for himself so when he got ready to retire he brought himself 2 corvettes (black and white). He shopped and got incredible deals on them.

Most people would be content with 1 corvette but his lid is so high that to 2 was the norm for him.

B) Visualize the life a successful sales career can give you - imagine the places you can visit, the items you can buy and the lifestyle you can afford your loved ones with financial success. See more for you than what is currently in front of you.

C) Dare to dream - dream big and see how your future can unfold.

Make The Word No Your Best Friend

You will never survive in a competitive sales environment if you cannot handle and deal with the word no. It is as common as word as any in our modern day language. It has been programmed into our minds from an early age and still lingers on in the mind of most.

Consider how we learned how to walk. Little children will climb over to a table, place their hands upon it and pull themselves into a standing position. They will look around for a few months, let go and take a few steps. Then they fall down. Do they quit? Do they tell themselves that failing to walk this time means they will not walk at all? Or do they crawl back to that table and try again? Children fall down lots of times before they finally get the hang of walking.

Consider what it took for them to get the courage to take that first step. Children start off on their backs getting love and attention for others. Then they learn how to roll over on their stomach. In that position they begin to learn how to crawl. At first they scoot along but in time they learn how to pull their legs under them, get on all 4 and crawl. This process can take weeks or even months to master. But these children are determined to get the hang of it.

Through continued efforts and hard work the child learns how to grab hold of things, stand up and walk, Now he is reaching for everything and the word he becomes very familiar with is "no". Don't touch this, stop it, I am going to spank you, he is so bad, etc. etc., etc. Negatives words create negative thoughts within him and without realizing it, the activity he once partook with unashamed resolve he must now stop it.

Most parents have no idea of how detrimental it is to associate the word "no" with activities that are positive. Learning to walk is positive. Exploring your environment is positive. Yes, there are dangers associated with children pulling things down on themselves or knocking things over. But the act of reaching for something higher is not bad; matter of fact, it is the very essence of success.

So reach for the stars. Try to accomplish more today than you did before. And resolve to never, ever give up, no matter how many "no's' you have to listen to. Reach for the stars. You may hit the moon.

Why Most Insurance Agents Succeed at Sales

Success in selling Insurance is not an accident. When you first start off it's hard but the more you learn about how to succeed at what you are doing, the easier it becomes.

Success and failure is not an accident. You don't fall into success nor do you fall into failure. Sadly more people walk into failure than they need to. It is my hope that this article will give you some steps you can take on the path to success in Insurance sales.

1) Set a sales goal - there is a ton of information available on goal setting so I won't address those in this article. Keep in mind that a goal is like the bull's-eye an archer aims for when he draws back his bow. You cannot hit a target you don't aim for. Let your sales goals reflect the targets you want to hit in your career.

2) Make a plan to reach that goal- break it down so that you know each day the activities you need to perform to hit your goal. For example, if you want to earn $100,000 a year you know that you need to make $2000 in commissions each week (taking 2 weeks off for vacation), which breaks down to $400/day and $50/hour. Each task that you perform must be equal to someone getting paid $50 for the job. See your time being worth $50/hour.

3) Control your activity to increase your productivity- In line with making a plan you must control your activity. If you spend 3 hours a day reading emails, listening to voicemail, mailing envelopes and taking coffee breaks, you are losing 3 hours a day which is $150/day, $750/week and $37,500 a year. Can you afford to lose $37,500 year to non-productivity? I cannot.

4) Stop making excuses for failure - Failure is not an option. When some agents are failing, they blame everyone but themselves. "It's the leads; it's the clients; it's because I have no support staff; it's because I have no money." Take 100 responsibilities for your actions. Failure is waiting for us all. Leave him at the bus stop.

5) See yourself successful - Finally, see yourself succeeding. Nothing causes more failure than a mental image of failure being acceptable and expected. Look instead at how much better your life can be if you hit your sales goals, achieve your income projections and have time to share your wealth with people you love and care for. Nothing in life is better than that!

How Do I Make Money Selling Insurance?

I have had the privilege through the years of working in various related fields. Based on this experience I would like to share with you how to make money selling Insurance.

Is it possible to make a good living selling? Yes. You can easily support yourself with a sales career if you can have enough business to generate the commission you need to live on. Can you make a good living selling Insurance? Yes as long as you can turn in enough policies each week to generate commissions.

Let me offer to you a few suggestions of what you need to put in place if you want to make money selling Insurance;

1) Become an expert in sales - In order to make consistent money in a sales career you must understand the process of sales. It all begins with the product. whatever product you choose to sell you must learn as much about it as you can. Then you can answer questions your prospects have.

Master the process of sales by knowing how to detect buying signals from a prospect, how to answer objections and how to close. You have to ask for the business you want and assume that prospects talk to you because they want to buy.

2) Become an expert in getting new prospects - the bloodline to any sales business is to have a steady flow of customers. Just like retail store will fail if no one comes in and buys their merchandise, as an agent you will fail unless you have a steady flow of new customers seeking to do business with you.

You have a variety of options available including purchasing leads from an outside lead source, use direct mailing, cold call, door knock, etc. It will all depend on the types of policies you sell and the type of clients your policy attracts. If you work with higher end clients who spend a lot for monthly premiums it's hard to have an appointment based on just dropping by. These clients need to set an appointment in order to hear your presentation.

3) Set realistic goals you can set to hit your income goals - you must determine how much money you need to make and how many sales it will take to reach your goal. Focus on doing the activities that will allow you to hit your goals and you will make enough money to do what you desire.

Plan on making money and you will if you execute a good plan.

Being a Successful Sales Agent

Insurance sales can be a most rewarding profession. it offers with it a great income potential, ability to be a part of an elite group of professionals and a chance to help may people secure their financial future through insurance products. This is a great place to be and not everyone can handle being in this position.

When a person decides to work in sales there is a mentality involved that is unlike anything seen in other professions. There are both great pressures in sales along with great rewards.

There are some essentials you must adopt in order to experience the benefits of this position. Those include;

1) An unwavering commitment to being the best - you have to see yourself as a professional. That means that you must embrace the concept of being a sales professional. You must believe in the company you work for. And you must believe in the products you provide.

2) The early bird gets the worm - we need to start our day off early. That means we need to get up and prepare ourselves each morning. Some do that through prayer. Some through meditation. We need to enter the day with mental preparation working to our benefit. The first 15 or 30 minutes you spend in mental preparation will result in increased sales and more money in your pocket.

3) Read, read and read some more - there is a lot of information on sales that can be derived from reading. Some of the greatest ideas on motivation have been revealed to the world through books (Success System That Never Fails, Think and Grow Rich, Seven Habits of Highly Successful People and Rich Dad, Poor Dad) titles that have impacted millions for the better. If you want to become a person who makes a difference you need to add to your knowledge. Applied knowledge will result in power for your sales career.

4) Prospect and set appointments - when it is all said and done, you must sell. That means you need to prospect every day and set as many appointments as you can. This can be hard and tedious but the only way salesman makes money is by selling. You cannot sell if you have no one to see. This is one of the hardest disciplines to develop but absolutely essential.

Love what you do; do what you love. And whatever you do, do it with all your might.

Sales Strategies for Life Insurance

In order to become very efficient selling insurance to the public agents need to have sales strategies they can use. This article was written to address some of those strategies so that they can be implemented in an agent's techniques.

1) Always prospect - It helps to keep a stack of business cards handy and to pass them out when it is appropriate. Most people do not like being sold and don't like being pestered by a sales person. But if you are in a setting where it is appropriate to share what you do then pass out that card.

Wherever you go each day you need to see if you are looking at a potential prospect. Many of the places you frequent to do your personal business is made up of people who would benefit from your products. Constantly look for prospects.

2) Use the Internet - It is essential to establish a web presence for yourself if you want to succeed in business. The company you represent will undoubtedly have their own website. When you prospect you should be directing people to your own website. This will allow you to include info about yourself and the product/services you offer.

Your website does not have to be expensive but it should be informative. In addition to sharing what products you offer you can also tell your readers a little about yourself. There can be a place where people can leave you their contact info so that you can reach them later.

3) Learn the Sales Process - Great salespeople are not great by accident. They have mastered the various techniques used to close sales. Some of these techniques include; Listen to your prospect. Don't talk yourself out of the sale. Ask questions so you can better understand your prospect. Always be closing. Use every opportunity to use closing statements such as, so how does this sound to you? Is there any reason you can't sign this agreement today? All I need for you now is a check. When do you want this order to be shipped?

4) Train, train, train - you need a combination of knowledge about your products and proficiency in applying the sales process. The better you are in these two areas, the more money you can make if you increase the number of prospects you see each week. Take advantage of every opportunity to learn your products and practice closing sales.

You Must Have Appointments To Sell

This article is going to delve into an aspect of selling that seems very obvious but unless it is approached with a positive and productive approach, it can mean the end to an otherwise promising sales career.

You must have appointments to sell. Period. If you don't have these appointments, your career is going nowhere.

Insurance sales is hard work. Many agents think you need to have great products to sell. So they focus on the carrier and those products which they think will dazzle prospects. What they fail to realize is this; you can sell a good appointment a bad plan but you can't sell a bad appointment a good plan.

Many insurance companies believe that training is the magic component to sales success. So they create mandatory sales curriculums which you must complete in order to work for them. What they fail to realize is that a trained monkey at a zoo won't get any bananas if there is no one there to offer him any.

Great products and great training are important. But if that was all it took to ensure your success, then many more agents would have sales success. No, you need those things but after you get them you can still fail. You need people to see on a daily and weekly basis in order to make it in this business. You need appointments.

Let's look at why appointments are the lifeline to a successful sales career;

1) You only make money when you sell a product - You are paid to sell. You can only sell when you are meeting with a prospect that has an interest in and the ability to afford your product.

2) You can only sell a product to a prospect - Having great products in your briefcase won't make you any money. Those products have to come out of your bag, get shown to a prospect and purchased by them.

3) You can only see a prospect when you set an appointment - you need to arrange to meet with prospects. In insurance lingo we call that an appointment. The more you go on, the greater your chances of closing on them and earning some money.

No appointments = no prospects =no money to agent.

My suggestion to you is to focus your thinking time on how to get appointments so that you can sit with prospects and sell your products.

Set weekly minimum appointments, work towards them and close those sales!

Don't Quit When You Can Win

If you have chosen to embark on a career in sales then you have chosen to take your life down a roller coaster ride. Sales are full of the ups and downs that make life exciting!

Failure is inherent with a career in sales. Most of the time you have to deal with people who don't like or need your product. There is always an objection waiting for you to overcome. The financial pressure caused by you not producing sales can be overwhelming. Add to this that most successful people are not happy when they fail and you have the perfect combination for wanting to quit.

Let me offer you some encouragement. Don't quit when you are working on your goal. You don't know if you will succeed with the very next blow. Stay on task, on course and watch what happens to the diligent.

IT WILL GET BETTER! Hard to believe but it's true. Things always look darkest before the dawn. There are times when it gets incredibly hard to go on and continue pushing. But we have to remember that life is in a constant state of flux and things always change. They go from bad to worse to better to good (not always in that order).

CHANGE IS GOOD! It may not look like it at the time, but change is a good thing. Consider how it was when man began to ride horses instead of walking everywhere. I know he must have felt relieved and a horse could travel farther and faster than he had done on foot. However in time we had the railroad train, automobile and airplane. These methods were all faster and carried man farther. People are always changing. So will you in your sales career. Don't neglect changes for they will help propel you to new heights.

QUITTERS NEVER WIN! Who remembers the guy who almost made it? The winner of the silver medal in the Olympics. The team who came in second best at the championship game? Although most of us forget their names the one thing we will remember is the person who quits. Coming in 2nd is very important because it means you tried your hardest to come in first. Not everyone will be a superstar but when you enter the game, stay in it no matter what.

WINNERS NEVER QUIT- Finally, in the words of Mr. Churchill, "never, ever, ever quit". Stay in the game. Keep going. In the end you will be a better person.

Professional Salesperson or Full Time Prospector?

When you accepted the position as an Insurance Sales Agent, did you see that as a choice to also become a professional in your field? Did you have images of earning an above average income, living an above average life and connecting with movers and shakers?

Sales is a professional position. A good agent will and should earn as much as a professional in many other fields. Insurance Sales Agents should hold their heads up and be proud of their profession.

I wonder why so many agents are not able to do that? What causes an agent to feel like they are doing a lot of work and yet receiving little to no pay for it?

Here is one of the reasons; instead of working as a professional sales agent, they work as professional prospectors.

What is a professional prospector? It is an agent who spends 80-90% of their time looking for that next appointment. Problem is none of us get paid to prospect; we get paid to sell. So how do so many agents fall into this trap? Consider the following;

1) Contrary to popular belief the successful agent does not spend the majority of his time prospecting. He is not on the phone making 100's of phone calls a day; he is not physically stuffing and mailing 100's of letters a week. He is not outside knocking on doors, walking the pavement and trying to convince someone to buy from him while he is going broke.

2) What professional agents do is realize they are paid to sell. You only make money when you turn in an application that gets approved. Prospecting is a means to an end but not the end. If you focus all of your attention on prospecting I can almost guarantee you will not last long in this business.

3) Prospecting is important. But how do you go about doing it? By working smarter and not harder. How much skill does it take to stuff a letter into an envelope and mail it? To pass out flyers on cars in a parking lot or in the doorways of the homes in a neighborhood? Some of these jobs can be done by a high school student.

4) Professionals have learned that they get paid the most by doing their profession. Doctors hire staff to draw blood, check your insurance, collect your fee for the visit, set appointments, etc. Doctors didn't spend all that time and money in school to do jobs that they can hire someone else to do. As a professional sales agent you will get paid the most when you do what you are licensed to do; sell insurance.

I know that when you first start off your budget is very limited and you have to do these things because no one else will. You may not be able to pay for these services. But if I could offer you a bit of advice; focus on your strengths (selling insurance) and staff to your weakness. Mentally position yourself to bring on help to do the things that you need to have done but should not be doing yourself.

Focus first on selling. Figure out how to use other available resources to prospect.

Effective Prospecting Methods

Salespeople who plan on being effective in their career need to focus on getting in front of as many qualified prospects as they can. The only way you can make any money as a salesperson is to make sales. The way to more sales is to see more prospects. Sales is a number game and the people who do best play the numbers well.

I have found that in order to make sales you need to understand the sales process. This is not some fly but the seat of your pants process. Instead it is structured and followed a definite path. The sales process takes the following into consideration;

1) Define who is the target market for your product - a 25 year old isn't going to flock to purchase $3000.00 in burial insurance. It is important to prospect for potential clients who need your product.

2) Create a need to make an immediate decision - the phrase that stalls more sales is "I need to think it over". The best way to close on a sale today is to help potential clients see that today is the best day to make a good decision.

3) Utilize marketing strategies to your advantage - Marketing is how you let the world know what you do. To effectively prospect we need to use marketing to our advantage. That means things like:

A) Mailers - although many people don't rely on mailing as they use to it is still a method that has some merits. Most mailers generate a 1-3% return but that beats getting nothing back.

B) Phone Calls - cold calling is not the most effective way to prospect but if you can get the names of people who fit your demographic profile and who have a need for your product then you can use the phone to make appointments.

C) Seminars - this is one of my favorite ways to get new prospects. Here you speak to a group, get them excited about your product and then close the sale one on one. Gives an agent a lot of bang for their buck. You don't have to have long seminars, just provide enough info to get people interested.

All the great sales people focus on sales. They understand prospecting is important but they know that in order to get paid, you must write business. Effective prospecting does that very well.

Surviving While Selling

Selling is a great career. Financially fulfilling, recognition from peers on a job well done, prizes for doing a good job and the list goes on. You can end up with a very flexible schedule and be able to do things many people only dream about.

But selling can also be one of the most depressing careers a person could ask for. Low or no sales, no money coming in, irate customers, clients who leave you and cancel their policies, you know what I am talking about. How do you survive the ups and downs that come with a selling career?

Let me offer some "food for thought" if you are serious about surviving in this path.

1) See this as a career, not just a job- when you view sales as a career you develop a long - term mentality. You may have to change the companies you work for and even the products. But you don't change what you do. Sales is sales. So you focus on helping customers achieve their financial goals through Insurance products.

2) See it as a business opportunity - when you have a job you go to work, do your job and go home. But when you have a business you work longer, think harder and constantly try to increase your bottom line while preserving your integrity (you don't become a thief to stay in business). A career in Insurance sales is no different. You have to put in time to think about your business. You have to identify what your business is and who is your customer (a Medicare Supplement customer is different from a single 25 year- old male looking for inexpensive insurance). You have to manage your activities to create income and monitor your expenses closely.

3) Create multiple streams of income - people who generate large sums of money always diversify. How many actors own a ton of real estate? How many businesses were started by people who already had a successful business? Use your wealth created through your sales career to invest in other income producing projects so that you can begin to enjoy multiple streams of income. It makes dealing with the sales ups and downs more bearable.

4) Set your own financial house in order - make sure you have adequate life, health and other insurance products in place on yourself. You must be a student of your own product. You must believe in the benefits owning

insurance will have on your own life. Nothing is more tragic than an Insurance agent who passes away and had no insurance on himself.

5) Begin each day with an attitude adjustment - Start each day in the right frame of mind. Tell yourself that you are successful, you will see many new customers today and you will make a sale. Look forward to making money every day you go to work.

6) Get use to hearing the word "No" each day- this word comes with being in sales. Get use to it! Each no brings you closer to your yes. So love hearing it.

Things to Avoid in Choosing An Insurance Company to Work For

How do you pick the right company to work for as an Insurance Agent? Although there is no sure fire way to pick the right company for you to work with, you need to look into how the company hires its Sales Agents, trains them and supports them.

Over 80% of the people who take a sales position with Insurance companies will be out of the business within the first year, mainly because of their inability to locate enough new customers to sustain a new career. When we see agents earning six figure incomes that represents less than 5% of the sales force. Insurance is a great field to be in but you have to be wise if you are choosing this as a career.

There are some things we need to avoid in choosing an Insurance company to work for.

1. A manager who wants you to contact all the members of your family to make sales. This puts you on the spot, creates an imposition for your family, and is no true test of your ability to find clients. You should be contacting your family last or when you feel comfortable.

2. A manager who puts you in a cubicle with a phone and gives you the phone book and tells you to start dialing. He needs to lead by example and teach you how to prospect. Just telling you to cold call is no way to start you on an insurance career.

3. Sits you in a conference room and asks you to watch training videos. This is the worse way to learn the business.

4. Wants you to go on appointments at night. There is no reason the prospect can't come to your office during the day. Going out at night is a thing of the past except for small companies. There will be times where you will meet working families at home in the evenings but as we enter into the 21st century we find that many people will make the time to meet when they feel it is important.

5. Working under a manager who also writes and gets leads to give to you. Sadly many of them will keep the good leads for themselves and give you the crap.

I believe a person committed to a sales profession can make a very comfortable living in Insurance sales. Just do your homework, connect to a company with good training and a culture for success; find ways to prospect successfully and take good care of yourself and your family.

Things to Look For in An Insurance Company You Want to Work For

There are things we need to look for in an insurance company we want to work for. Insurance sales is a very hard position and if you want to enter into a place where you can earn regular, consistent income which is enough to support your lifestyle, you cannot just work anywhere.

Look at some of the characteristics you should pay close attention to when seeking employment;

1. Train as possible and read every book you can find on risk management, human life value, how insurance works, qualified plans, retirement planning, estate planning, Social Security, investment planning, and how life insurance improves and enhances these items. The more you understand these concepts the better you will be at your job.

2. Read everything you can about marketing, sales, how to attract clients, communication skills, body language and making presentations. The more you can learn about how this business of sales works the better you will be at performing it. If you read just one book a month over a 5 year period on the same subject, at the end of that time you will know more about that subject than 90% of the general public.

3. Think of all the reasons you would or should not buy insurance and then develop responses that overcome these objections before they come up. Hearing no, I want to think about it, can we do it later, etc. is customary in insurance sales. In order to do well in Insurance you must be able to handle objections.

4. Join every organization you feel you can contribute to. By being an active member you will not only make friends and meet potential associates but you will increase your exposure as an expert in your field. Nothing carries a career farther than being regarded as an expert in your field.

5. Work in an office that exudes positive mental attitudes. The more you can experience a positive atmosphere the higher you will climb. Negative people produce negative thoughts that can kill your dreams. Instead let the positive perspective of others propel you to heights not thought of. You can soar as an agent once you really believe it's possible.

This is a very rewarding field, but it is also very difficult. On average, 75% of those who start do not last more than a few years. That is because of little to no training, limited knowledge and communication skills. Don't be a casualty.

Should I Be A Captive or Non Captive Agent

When you enter into the Insurance sales field you have to ask yourself this question at some time in your career; should I be a captive or non- captive agent?

A captive agent is one who works for one company and agrees to only sell their products. A non-captive agent can represent more than one company and offer a variety of products. There are agents who have experienced success using both methods. You have to decide for yourself which direction you want to take your business in.

A captive agent will sign on with a company, go through their training and become proficient in selling their products. Many times captive companies focus on a particular niche in the marketplace although they may have a menu of products customers can choose from. Some of these companies even offer their agents a beginning salary or guarantee to get them going in the Insurance field.

There are advantages to the captive agent. You get to focus on and become very proficient with how your company works. You tend to work with the same support staff, underwriters and agents. You have a manager you report to. Many times you even have regular hours to go into the office each week.

Disadvantages include; you have to focus only on your company's products. If your company doesn't offer universal life products, you can't sell them. It's very hard as a captive agent to deal with every client you come across because you are limited in your product offerings. It's like being in the restaurant business; nobody goes to Kentucky Fried Chicken for tacos. Managers can sometimes forget that you are not really employees but independent contractors and make requirements of you that only a W-2 employee has to follow. Finally, your commissions may be less in a captive contract.

There are advantages to being a non-captive agent. You get to create your own menu of products you want to offer to your clients. You can get larger shares of the commissions because you are not a real expense to the insurance company.

They can afford to give you more because you only make money when you send them business. You can determine which clients in the marketplace you want to focus on and contract with those companies to offer their products. You don't have expected office hours.

Disadvantages include; you don't have a manager to support you in your business. Many times you will feel you are on your own and you would be right. You may not have the proper contracts in place to service your clients or you may have the wrong contracts (products you don't sell anyway).

It will all depend on how you want to structure your business. Either option of captive or non-captive can work.

Find out what fits best for you.

The Lies Told To Agents About Leads

Agents must meet prospects and make presentations in order to get sales. Typically these presentations are the result of working leads. The quality of those leads should be of the utmost importance to any agent who wants to succeed in this business.

Sadly many agents are told lies about the leads they receive. This article is intended to expose some of the lies agents hear from lead sources;

1) These leads are exclusive - agents many times believe that they are the only one working a lead. Although this may be true some of the time, most leads are shared. You can have as many as 3-4 other agents calling on your leads. This is evidenced by the fact that when you call a lead you just got, chances are you are not the first agent to call them that day.

2) These leads are fresh - if you can call leads shortly after they have responded to the marketing inquiry you increase your chances of converting People tend to forget the longer it takes an agent to get back to them. Calling old leads many times is a waste of time.

3) We close _____% of these leads - the closing ratio can be highly subjective. I have purchased leads based on the stated ratios and not always seen the results promised. As an agent you feel like you are always doing something wrong when you don't get appointments. Sometimes the calls you are making are not worth the effort.

4) We make no money on selling you these leads - a classic comment made by many Insurance companies. The question I would consider is this; if companies are producing leads for agents at cost, why are they so expensive? And how can they afford to have these huge prospecting generation operations if there is no money to be made in leads?

Remember there are companies out there who only make money from selling leads and they cost as much (sometimes less) than what an Insurance company offers to their agents. Lead generation is big business and companies offer these to agents because they know this is another stream of income to them.

Do good quality leads cost money to secure? Yes. They require work, planning and focus to acquire. If you desire to be an effective agent who makes good money, focus on getting the best you can purchase.

Myths about Leads

The biggest problem for a Sales Agent is finding enough qualified prospects to offer their products to. Insurance companies attempt to solve that problem by offering agents a lead program.

This is how it typically works;

1) Agencies advertise that they have leads for agents. Typically they are either direct mail or telemarketing.

2) Agencies either advance leads to their agents or charge them as they are received or they require them to pay upfront.

Sounds like a real plan. Yet this plan has within it inherent faults that agents need to be more aware of.

1) Costs - its not uncommon for agencies to charge anywhere from $2 (cold leads) to $60 for a hot lead.

2) Quality - although agents pay for leads the truth is many leads purchased are truly a waste of time

3) Type - these leads can allow an agent to make a good living. But agencies don't makes good leads available without an agent jumping through a lot of hoops to get them. Have you ever asked yourself "why"?

it is very, very difficult to find a qualified prospect that can purchase an insurance policy from you today. Insurance companies know that. So they work hard to have agents find those prospects for them. For many companies promising to provide leads is just a way to get new agents through the door. Then by having agents sell their family and friends these same companies can increase their client base at the expense of the agent.

So what is the solution? Is my goal to put down Insurance companies? No. Instead I think that agents need to know that if you play the lead game chances are your career will lead you to making a change.

Here are some ways to try to not fall into the lies told about leads;

1) Pay attention to the actual cost of the lead - leads can be expensive but you don't want to pay for the cost it took someone else to get the leads. You want to pay for a good lead which can lead to a sale.

2) All leads are not created equal - I got some leads and had a professional telemarketer call them to set appointments for me. She was so frustrated with the quality of leads I gave her that she quit. Her comment to me was "I can't waste my time calling people who have not expressed any prior interest at all in your product. It's a total waste of time calling these leads." What was sad is these leads represented leads I had purchased so I was out of the money to buy them and they resulted in no sales.

3) Don't fall into the trap of thinking all leads have the potential of being good. Some leads are a total waste of time (such as trying to sell senior citizens on a fixed income a high premium policy plan.

Good Leads Will Lead You To Sales Success

Leads are the lifeline of any Insurance business. With them you can call, mail and find prospects who want to purchase your product. Without them you will be out of business in a short period of time.

There are different types of leads and great agents strive to surround themselves with as many good leads as possible. These include;

1) Cold leads - these leads are to people who have expressed no prior interest in your product and the agent has no prior knowledge that they will have an interest. We use to call people from the white pages and ask them if they had thought about purchasing insurance (I don't recommend this method to anyone who wants to make the best use of their time). You can get business from them but you will need to go through hundreds, maybe thousands to find that 1 or two percent.

2) Warm leads - these leads are to people who may have an interest in your product but more importantly they have a relationship either with the agent or someone the agent knows. A lot of insurance companies hire new agents for the sole purpose of gaining access to their warm market (mother, father, sister, brother, relatives, friends that an agent knows). They require the agent to sell his warm market first before they allow him to work for him.

Most agents who fall for this find that unless they learn how to really sell insurance, once their warm market dries up, they are out of business. Agents need to learn how to get a fresh supply of new prospects daily.

It is OK to work with warm leads provided they really want your product and are not buying just because you have a relationship with them.

3) Hot leads - these people have expressed an interest in the agent's products and will meet with him to discuss purchasing the product. these are the best leads to have.

Hot leads can be; working at a trade show, sharing what you do and having people fill out a card to have you come and present to them. It can be responding to people who either call you or go to your website and ask for information when they know the information includes you contacting them

Hot leads are also referrals you get where the person you got the referral from has actually called them and told them you would be contacting them.

Make it a habit to go after good leads in your sales career. You will get paid a lot faster if you do.

I Am Ready to Quit Selling Insurance

If you have made a decision to build a career selling insurance products, congratulations. You have made a choice that can positively impact your future, your finances and your family.

I wish I didn't have to tell you but you have also made a decision to introduce one of the hardest experiences you will have in your life.

Disappointment. And why am I saying that?

Because the longer you stay in this business the more likely you will be to say "I am ready to quit selling insurance". But why? Why do well over 80% of the agents that get their license and work for insurance companies quit within the first year? Let me give you a few reasons to consider:

1) Rejection by potential customers - you will need thick skin to make it in this business because you will hear the phrase "no thank you" so many times you will begin to think it's your first name. People don't typically run out to buy insurance. They have to be convinced that it is something they should seriously consider now. The one customer who knows for sure insurance is important is the person who has experienced firsthand either death or illness with no insurance. That will not be the majority of your customers so they will say no often. Get us to it!

2) Financial Insufficiency - most insurance companies are extremely rich. A large part of that reason is they are an industry that gets most of their business from salespeople but they guarantee no wages. If a salesman doesn't make a sale, he doesn't get paid. This means that as a salesman you must have the financial resources to go to work every day, keep your car running, pay for a phone service, and wash your clothes so you look nice in front of customers, pay your household bills and eat while not getting a dime for your efforts. Most of us cannot afford to go to work every day and handle the expenses of living with no money coming in.

On some policies you can get paid rather quickly while others take weeks. So a new agent is expected to do all he has to in order to write and submit business. Yet he gets no money. It's not long before he is out of the insurance business and taking a job with more financial stability.

3) Managerial Incompetence - one of the hardest challenges for a sale agent is to be working under an incompetent manager. Many times insurance companies promote managers from salesmen who did well in sales. However sales and management are two different animals. You can be an excellent salesman but not know the first thing about management. I have worked under managers who thought their job was to push you to sell. Salesmen need guidance in their careers to keep them focused on the goal; make money as quickly as possible.

Don't quit. Find out how to win and fight until you do.

Decide To Make A Difference in Sales

A sales career is a great decision. With it we can reach out to the masses and offer products that not only can change someone's financial future but prepare them to deal with the accidents that happen to us all in life.

My challenge to you today is to decide; decide on what kind of career you will have in Insurance sales.

You can become an agent that is focused on making money. Your commission could be the overriding factor in all of your customer dealings. Yes you have a family, bills and obligations. You have a lifestyle you want to continue and goals to achieve.

As a result of this kind of focus people get sold products they don't need. They get policies they can't afford to keep. All because this "UL" policy pays a higher commission than this "term" policy. Who cares what is best for the customer, right? It's the salesperson we must be more concerned about.

No! A thousand times no!

When a sales career moves strictly into the money potential found in a sale, salespeople can lose the reason why they got into the career in the first place. That is one of the reasons I believe it's not always in an agents best interest to start him off selling his family and friends. Many new agents use the relationships they have established in the past to further their endeavors in insurance. They set appointments and sell people they have a prior relationship with.

There is nothing wrong with selling family and friends who have a need for your product (don't believe that everyone needs what you sell; I don't need maternity insurance at this time). There is something wrong when the only reason a new agent sells his family and friends is to generate commissions for himself. If an agent comes into this business looking to use his family and friends for his own personal benefit, what hope is there for the new prospects he will meet?

Decide to make a difference in sales. Instead of selling people products based on your potential commission, sell them what they need and want. Show them how the plans you propose can meet those needs and wants.

Then when you close the sale and collect a check you can be assured that you have not only given them what they need but what is best for them. These policies are hard for another agent to come in and replace.

Sad to say, there are agents who are so concerned about getting paid that they go in and replace good policies a client already has. If your client took out a cash value policy 10 years ago and now their health is bad but you want to sell them a new fully underwritten policy because you believe the cash value in their present policy will pay for the new one, ask yourself this question; is it truly best for this client, under these conditions? If the answer is no, then please reconsider your actions.

Decide to be a professional in this business; decide to do what's best for your client first. Money always follows when we do the right things.

Make It Happen For Your Future

When a person takes a job in Insurance Sales the initial belief is "I can do this". You hear about how your company's products help people, how great the office support is, how much money can be earned, etc.(who ever recruits and says the products are lame and the office support does not exist?)

It is great to have support in these areas. However there is a mentality you need to keep in mind when it comes to working with any Insurance company; you have to "make it happen." What do I mean by that? Consider the following;

1) You have to prospect for your next deal - Insurance companies provide tools but just like a carpenter needs to work to build a house, you must take the tools and work to build your book of business house.

2) You have to review conditions on each case - I have had clients come up with all kinds of excuses as to why they are dragging their feet to do what they need to. It may be a phone interview or a para-med exam. As the writing agent you need to stay on top of what is going on with your clients.

3) You have to watch your commissions - once a case is approved you had better check to make sure your commissions are paid to you as agreed for the amount you agreed upon.

It's your future. Only you really care about your goals. Sure, others may know those goals and even support them but in the end, it's up to you. You must make it happen.

Here are some tips on how to do just that;

1) Take personal responsibility. It's your future, your family's happiness and your finances at stake. So you get up and make it a point to give it your all each day.

2) Operate from a plan - don't hit the day hoping something will stick. Be very deliberate in your quest for success at your new endeavor. Organize your daily activities to maximize your production.

3) Delegate your weaknesses - to make it happen you must play to your strengths. Just like an athlete works to do what he does best to win a game (shoot free throws, run the football or hit the next pitch) you must position yourself to do the same. Spend no time trying to get better at what you are no good at. Instead, live in your strengths.

Salesperson or Sales Manager: Which Career Should You Pick

Sales is a wonderful position. If you choose to be involved in it you can decide to become either a salesperson or a sales manager. But how do you decide which position is best for you. Let us look more closely at what each position is and what it takes to be successful in each.

Sales - you have the responsibility of presenting your products to the public. In order to do this successfully you need to know your product, know your client and know how to sell. Just because you offer something people need and probably want does not mean they will purchase from you.

What makes a good salesperson is to have someone who can consistently provide sales to your company; they are nice to your customers and build a referral base because of how well they do their job. Sales is the backbone of American companies and without it, most corporations would crumble and fall by the wayside.

For the person who likes working with different people each day, who wants some control over their income and to be rewarded for their efforts, a sales career could be right up your alley.

Sales Managers - this role seems to have some confusion for many people. I have had managers in the past who felt like they were salespeople who managed instead of managers who had sales people. There is a big difference.

A good sales manager knows their job is to manage the sales people under them. They need to make sure their agents have all the tools they need to do their job, engaging in making sure their staff is trained in both sales and product knowledge and helps them to get paid as quickly as possible on all submitted business. When managers run around constantly trying to outsell their sales people you don't have a manager; you have a confused agent trying to wear two hats and not really succeeding as well as they could if they would focus on one position.

That is the real key to making it either as a salesperson or as a manager; focus. Why do you do what you do? Where should you be spending the majority of your time?

If you are in sales, I can tell you that all the other activities you do should be leading to a sales opportunity because that is the only way you will make money. If you are in management you should be mentoring and training your staff to become as great as they can be. That is the acid test of a truly great manager.

I don't know which position suits you best. But please, pick one and become the best at it you can.

How to Get and Close More Sales

To be an effective salesperson you need to be able to get in front of people, share your product and help people meet their needs by possessing what you have to sell. Don't make the mistake of thinking that you only need to be in front of people who have expressed a prior need. Such thinking can kill your Insurance sales career.

Why? Because there is a small number of people who express a need for insurance. Given the number of agents out there trying to meet with those people it's fair to say that these potential clients are being bombarded. I know it makes sense to go after the warm crowd (those who won't hang up initially if they initiated the call or sent in a mailer). These actually are good leads. The problem for most agents is there are not enough to go around.

If you happen to work for an Insurance company that has writing managers it's fair to assume that they will be dealing with the hot and warm leads that come to your company. These include call ins, walk ins and leads where the person who sent it in has an immediate desire to see an agent. But for the average agent you must be ready to find ways to reach people without waiting for those types of leads.

When you purchase leads those leads typically are sold to 3 or 4 agents at the same time you get them so you are racing to get the call in as fast as possible. Lead companies tell you upfront they sell these same leads to multiple agents as a way to make optimum profits from each lead they generate. Is it fair? No. But is it reality? Yes.

If you want more sales you have to convert the group of people who have not expressed a desire to get insurance. This means we have to get people to first look at insurance, then listen to the benefits, then hear a sale close and make a decision. Much like the grocery store which never advertises all the products they have to offer but they advertise enough to get people to come in and see what they have to offer. We have to do the same thing.

I wish I could offer you an easy way to make money when you are in Insurance sales. But that would be a lie. Insurance sales are hard and in order to make it, you have to find new prospects.

I wish you well in your search.

The Truth About Leads and Lists

The key to being a successful agent is not what many agents are taught. Some believe its training; the more product knowledge you have the better you will be. Others believe its products; you need to represent companies with great companies. I believe the key component to an agent's success is the effectiveness of his prospecting for potential clients.

There is a big difference between sales and marketing. Sales is a process that moves a client to make a decision. Marketing is what exposes your company and its products to the world. The better a company is at marketing itself, the more sales it will have. Look at some of the companies that market effectively today (such as McDonalds, GEICO and Progressive to name a few) and see how their sales are a direct reflection of their marketing efforts.

Through marketing Insurance companies produce leads. I have written a few articles on leads so I won't repeat the info here. A lead is when a potential client inquires about your company or your product and an agent contacts them to answer their questions and hopefully get a chance to make a sales presentation. This has proven to be a very effective method of reaching new clients.

Although many insurance companies say they have "leads" what they really have is lists. When I trained real estate agents in prospecting we would identify the area we wanted to list houses for sale, get lists of the homeowner in the area and call them with a simple script; "my name is Joe Blank and I work for Real Estate Company. Have you thought about selling your house either now or in the near future," Depending on the answer we would respond accordingly.

When agents call from lists they are in essence doing the same thing. Yes you have demographic info and you can call to give them a pitch about your company. But this is not a lead because those customers did not call in or mail in for info. Statistically the ratio of people who agree to an appointment from such a call is dismally small (1-2 % if you are good). This means that most agents will get very frustrated calling these people who mainly have no interest in getting with a sales agent.

To become more effective in your insurance career, try to call leads for appointment and lists when you want to prospect because you have free time. If you try to make a living off of just lists, I can guarantee your insurance career will be filled with many frustrating days, low sales totals and a need to find a more financially rewarding job.

Why Is My Sales Career So Unsuccessful

People typically get into a sales career in order to accomplish some personal goals; high income, recognition, freedom, lifestyle of the rich and famous, etc. Sales can truly be a great career if a good agent can find a good company to work for.

Yet if sales has the potential to be such a great career, why do so many agents have to leave their sales jobs? Agents transfer companies often. When you check the available ads you will find many insurance companies constantly looking for new agents. On the outside it would appear that these agents cannot do business, don't work hard enough, and have not had enough training, etc. The companies tend to just look for new agents instead of addressing why the currently hired agents are not successful.

I do believe there can be a variety of reasons why agents have not found the success they could have and do deserve in sales. See if any of these resonate within you;

1) Agents don't understand that selling insurance is a business - In a business the bottom line is profits; if you fail to make a profit, you fail to prosper. Agents must look at the commission structure they are offered to make sure the commission they earn will give them a return on the investment they must make in order to secure a sale (gas to get to appointments, cell phone for calls, marketing materials, etc.). It's not about what commission you are promised; it's about how much profit you have left after spending money to do sales.

2) Agents trust the lead sources insurance companies give to them- For a new agent they can sometimes be very gullible when it comes to leads. Give them a page with names on it, tell agents that "on average our agents set 3 appointments for every 10 names we give them" and agents start counting their sales. But not all leads are equal. A cold lead is one where the person has not asked for your product so when you contact them the chances of them saying yes can be as low as 1%. Agents need to work leads where people have requested info.

3) Agents cannot handle the freedom of setting their own schedules - Kills many people use to 9 to 5 jobs. You must be disciplined to get up and work.

4) Companies hire agents to do their advertising for them - Many times companies only advertisement is the agent contacting the public. Makes an agent's job very hard.

Success is highly possible in a sales career. You must work hard and work for a company that truly understands how to market their services to this business savvy community of consumers.

Working In Sales Full Time For Free

Salespeople earn more money than most people in other professions. It is not uncommon to find sales people with six figure incomes and if you are in sales or upper management you may see a seven figure income.

On the other hand, there are minimum wage workers who earn more than some salespeople. You can go totally broke with a sales position.

How can this be? I believe it is because some sales people have embraced the lie of working in sales full time for free.

When you are in sales you have to be more disciplined than the hourly worker. If not you will not get paid. Look at why people don't get paid in sales:

1) **Failure to expect to make a sale** - if you are going to see a potential sales client then you should expect to close the sale. There are times when sales people go on appointments and make a presentation only to not make a sale. No one can guarantee a sale all the time but we must expect to sell if we hope to make regular sales.

2) **Failure to prospect regularly** - we must speak to new people constantly to keep the flow of potential customers coming in. Failure to prospect means we run the risk of having no new clients. We need to always focus on getting new clients to fill our pipeline.

3) **Failure to plan and execute directly** - it's been said "plan your work and then work your plan". It can become tedious but if you really want to be successful then you have to take time to plan. I find that even after coming home and calling it a day I have to spend a few minutes reviewing what I need to do for tomorrow. This gets my mind ready to go to sleep and dream up ways to be productive. Make a good plan that will help you reach your goals. Then execute it.

4) **Failure to see sales as a profession position** - don't buy into the lie that this is not a real profession. It is and the more you embrace it professionally, the more it will pay you back as such. Is it easy? No. But is it worth it? Yes.

If you are going to devote your time to doing sales, then don't settle for minimum wage as to reflect what you are worth. Earn your value in sales.

Prospecting and Sales Appointments Are the Key to Success

I have been in sales for over 10 years. During that time I have sold tangibles (appliances, real estate) and intangibles (insurance, consulting). Regardless of the products you sell the method to make sells doesn't change. You must prospect, set appointments, give presentations and close sales. This is commonly referred to as the sales process.

It is hard to become a great salesperson with a dependable income stream unless you develop a system to do just that. Fortunately such a system exists if you get your information and plug it in. Let us see how to use this info and increase our sales;

1) Prospecting - the hardest part of the sales process for many salespeople. The reason is you have to prospect a lot of potential clients before you can get to the ones who will purchase your product. To become more effective at prospecting focus on potential clients first. These are people who fit your present customer criteria. The goal is to prospect for people who have a good chance of saying yes to your proposal.

2) Setting appointments - this is a necessary skill. Prospecting will do you little good if you do not set appointments. When you do this effectively you make your prospecting efforts pay off. You cannot sell unless you make an appointment to show your products and services.

3) Giving presentations - the heart of every sale. The quality of your presentation and your proficiency of sharing it with others will directly impact your sales. As a representative you must become an expert at giving your presentation. You must know your product inside and out, be able to answer questions and have a firm grasp of the sales cycle.

4) Closing sales - even with great prospecting, the ability to set appointments and giving great presentations, if you cannot close you will not make any money. Closing sales is when you ask the prospect to make a decision to purchase. You ask for the money and get the signatures. There are many ways to get to this point but unless you can 'close the sale" you won't get paid.

The key to success in a sales career is being able to engage in the activities that will increase your sales. These four pointers outlined in this article give you the nuts and bolts you need to be able to make good sales decisions.

Don't Waste Time When You Are Prospecting

I would love to tell you that sales training in the Insurance industry is geared towards making agents successful. Although you would think this to be true the reality is most sales training that is geared towards getting you business is a waste of time.

Why do I say that? Consider these statements:

1) Get use to hearing more the word "no"

2) You have to knock on a lot of doors to reach your goal

3) If you want to make a lot of money in sales you have to focus on cold calling

There is some truth in these statements. But let me offer some insights into the reality of what these statements mean to the salesman.

1) If you get us to the word "no" then you have to get use to failing. Every sales call you go on you need to expect to hear a "yes". Negativity does nothing when you goal is to generate positive results. How can an agent get excited about hearing the word "no"? Who can keep getting up and taking the abuse of being told no the majority of each day?

I want to offer you an alternative; Instead of looking for more "no's" how about looking for people who can offer you a "yes"? If you are a shoe salesman trying to sell shoes to Indians who don't wear shoes, you are asking for a very negative experience. But if you sell shoes to women who tend to buy a fair share of shoes, you may hear "yes".

2) I am not knocking on doors to look for new business. I am addressing the foolishness of going out into the marketplace just hoping you will find a suitable client. That is not true. As agents you must market your product to potential clients who either already have your product or would purchase if they could see the benefit. To think that every person needs our product is certainly old school thinking.

3) Cold calling needs to change. Some companies use cold calling as a way to avoid spending money on advertising and marketing, using agents to get their product out to the public. Agents should always look for new prospects. But you must focus on finding people who do, can or will use your product.

Years ago I worked for a company that sold dictionaries. They would put a group of us in a van, drop us off in a suburban area and have us go door to door asking people to purchase our dictionary. The lie they told us was "everyone who speaks needs a dictionary." I was young and dumb. That is not the way to sell dictionaries and we all failed as salesmen to earn any real income.

Prospect effectively.

Very Archaic Hiring Practices

Insurance is a very profitable business and sales agents can make a ton of money. People need insurance so the market is not shrinking but growing as the population enlarges.

What amazes me is the hiring practices for most Insurance companies have not changed even though we are in a new century. Let me explain the typical way an Insurance company hires, trains and loses 80% of their first year agents.

1) A cattle call goes out to anyone with an insurance license or the willingness to obtain one - Insurance companies hit all the hiring venues to find people who have sales experience or wish to get into a sales position.

2) A presentation is given where the top earners and income potential are portrayed - it is very hard to listen to a presentation and hear about people earning hundreds of thousands of dollars when the average wage for a family of 4 is not $50,000. Add to that all the toys you can purchase when you earn a lot of income and the lifestyle is hard to not envy. Insurance companies use wealth to lure people into a sales position.

3) New agents are subjected to a lot of training - this is both a good and bad thing. Most companies have a canned presentation which they say results in the majority of their sales. Yet a lot of the veteran agents don't use the presentation because they focus more on a warm market. These people don't need the presentation new agents are taught.

4) Once trained, new agents are expected to go out and produce - With the heavy emphasis on training, many companies believe that once an agent finishes training he has all he needs to be successful. But the truth is, working for anyone seldom comes with no expenses. Yes new agents are trained. But they have two expenses to contend with every day; their normal living expenses and the business expenses they incur from working this job. If agents don't generate income in a relatively short period of time they run the risk of being in a financial hole trying to work in Insurance.

5) Most agents only write business on themselves and their friends, then their business dries up - I consider this to be a bad decision. Yes, if you need insurance and you sell it, you should buy it from yourself. But if you only buy because of the new job then you are not truly a salesman. Like any business you will only survive in sales if you can generate enough activity from the public to support yourself.

It's time to invest in new agents with much more than training. Cover the cost of doing business so agents have a fair chance of succeeding.

Sale Your Way to Financial Success

It is possible to sale your way to financial success. That is the good news.

It is highly improbable you will sale your way to financial success. That is the real news.

Why would I say it's "highly improbable". you will sale your way to financial success? Because the way most sales programs are set up through insurance companies a new agent has to break free from the pack in order to find financial success.

Let me explain. Almost every company has some type of training in place. This is essential to being successful. However, if all an agent needed was to be trained, then companies would be filled with productive agents. However that is not the truth. No matter what you chosen field of endeavor, you will need a lot more than training if you want to become a star in your career.

Common misconceptions to finding financial success as an agent include;

1) All you need to do is memorize and deliver our sales presentation- there is a lot of truth to that but each client you meet is different. You must be flexible enough to adapt your presentation to meet your clients' needs. This thought that every situation requires the same presentation will cause a new agent to fail.

2) If you fail, it's because you are not following our system - this is a very arrogant statement. It assumes that the system in place is foolproof. Anyone who has watched what has happened to big businesses over the years can tell you otherwise. Ask Enron, Circuit City and Lehman Brothers if doing things in the way they worked before has worked out for them.

3) Many companies have not entered into the 21st century - companies have to change if they hope to be successful. Some companies don't have their presentations on laptops or IPads, they still use paper sheets to figure rates and insist on using one method to get new clients. Clearly over 50% of the population searches for insurance online and if you fail to have a presence there, you are missing the boat.

4) Most sales trainers don't produce productive agents -lastly, the way to tell if your trainer is any good is to see how many productive agents they have produced. If you are not able to sale at a consistent high level yourself how can you reproduce that in other agents. Trainers must be able to show new agents how to get off to a fast start and make money as fast as possible.

Take control over your sales career. Don't allow anyone or anything to stand in the way of your dream of becoming a productive agent. Become an agent that cares for his clients.

Transforming Into a Sales Professional

It is one thing to be a salesperson. It is quite another to become a sales professional.

What is the difference? A salesperson sells. They talk to potential clients, give presentations and help those clients make a decision regarding their products. Many times when a sale closes, the salesperson moves on to the next potential client.

A sales professional does the same things with a few differences. Those differences include;

1) They turn potential clients into new clients who they follow up with - a sale is not the end for a sales professional; it is the beginning of a relationship that will hopefully last for years. They know the hardest customer to acquire is a new one so they make sure they hold on to their old ones.

2) They build a solid referral base from past clients - when you do a good job you can ask for referrals. Those who are looking to become sales professionals must develop the habit of asking current clients for new potential clients. A satisfied customer has no problem referring when the service was good.

3) They excel at customer service - this is how they can ask for referrals. They excel at making sure all customer problems are addressed and dealt with. This gives them an opportunity to show that they can not only write business but handle what was written. Satisfied customers brag to their friends.

4) They see themselves just as professional as a doctor or attorney - this is a major key difference in becoming a professional. When you deal with people who have paid the price to learn their trade, get licensed in their trade, study their trade and excel in it, you are looking at a professional. Sales professionals expect to be talked to and treated with the same respect we have for our doctors and attorneys.

They dress the part. They talk the part. They look the part.

5) They look to earn professional wages for their services - given all the above you can see why a true sales professional expects to earn a great wage. Would any attorney go to law school and pass the bar to earn $35,000 a year? How about a doctor who earns $13 an hour? Not going to happen.

A $100,000 a year income earner makes $51.28 an hour. A $25,000 a year income earner makes $128.21 an hour.

Where does your mentality lie when it comes to the income you should be making? I hope you are striving to not only be viewed as a Sales Professional but to earn like one as well.

How To Train A Sales Agent To Be Effective

Insurance companies focus a lot of their attention on recruiting new agents. The reason is very simple; agents account for the majority of new business Insurance companies write.

Given that new agent productivity is paramount to continued success it would seem that training programs that ensure that would abound in most Insurance companies. Sadly that is not the way it is. Even to this day there is an incredible amount of turnover in new agents due to their inability to become productive.

Who would want a full time sales position that pays $20,000 a year? When you consider all of the expenses of being in a commission position along with the difficulty of getting new clients a person who settles for what they could earn full time working in retail or a restaurant should seriously consider a new career. I am not knocking what people in retail or the restaurant industry go through. But being in full time sales is very hard. It makes more sense to earn an above average income since you will be dealing with above average job stress.

That being the case let me share with you a method to train new agents for optimum efficiency as early as possible.

1) Make sure agent has some product training prior to hitting the streets - this can be done in classroom, online or in a group setting. Agent must have a basic understanding of the products his company offers along with learning the presentation of his company.

2) New agents need to see experienced agents set appointments - when you bring on a new agent he needs to spend some time watching experienced agents prospect and set appointments. Don't have him watch a new agent work warm leads, orphan leads or anything that this new agent won't be calling on. If he is expected to get appointments from cold calling, then he needs to see someone make those calls and have success. If he is going to go and prospect in the streets he needs to see it done by example from an experienced agent.

3) New agents need to watch a presentation, take notes and not say a word - show him how it is done from start to finish with no interruptions.

4) Have new agent participate in presentation- let him do some parts of the presentation and trainer can observe and help out.

5) At end of day let agent explain to other agents what he learned from his experience

6) Repeat this process only let new agent do entire presentation. Then trainer can critique.

Repetition is the mother of learning.

It Is Possible to Make Real Money in Insurance Sales

If you desire to have a successful career in Insurance it is definitely possible. The key is to understand what you need in your career in order to experience the success you deserve.

Yes, I said you deserve it! Failure is not an option and success is not an accident. For the person who wishes to really have all the benefits a sales career can offer you need to succeed. You must purpose in your heart to have all that you are capable of.

Here are a few things you will need to incorporate into your success plan to achieve the goals you want;

1) Be very clear as to what you want from your Insurance sales position - Although this can be a very lucrative position financially it is very easy to go broke selling insurance. You must be very clear as to what you are looking for when it comes to selling and have clear goals that you track daily (yes I said daily). The key to sales is not just making sales but getting paid (see number two).

2) You must ensure you get paid on time for your sales activities - nothing hurts more than to be out there doing your job selling and turning in business only having to wait indefinitely before being paid. You have to make sure that you know the timeline for getting policies issued and how long you have to wait to be paid;. Typically the non-medical plans issue much faster than the fully underwritten ones.

3) Think about the people you serve first, not your commissions - as an agent it is so easy to think about getting paid. The focus for success is to think about the people you are serving with your insurance products and try to help as many people as you can. In order for you to experience the success you want you need to focus on helping people get what they want. The more people you help, the more success you will have in your career.

4) Give back as you get more - finally, don't allow success to stop with you. Reach out to the less fortunate. Give to that poor person you see on the streets. Find charities you can donate both time and money to. Let the world be a better place because you are in it. Freely you received a great career; freely give back.

The Way to Build More Sales Quickly

It is very easy to fail in sales. If you fail to prospect for new potential clients, if you fail to give your sales presentation to others and if you fail to close, you will fail in sales. But there is no reason to fail when succeeding is easier. Sounds like it is not possible but it is.

In order to gain new prospects (which is the foundation for more sales because without prospects, you will have no presentations) you must be able to persuade people to listen to whatever approach you use to reach them. I want to share with you 4 ways to become better at getting people to want to listen to you so that you can make them a potential prospect.

A) Attention- Most people are terrible listeners. In order to gain the trust from a potential prospect you must pay attention to what they are saying. The problem with communication among many people today is that we are so busy planning our response that we can't focus on what the other person is saying. To get more prospects sincerely pay attention to what they are saying.

B) Understanding- After you have given attention you must show understanding. Steven Covey wrote in the 7 Habits of Highly Successful People that we should "seek first to understand, then to be understood". To move people to want to become clients, we have to understand where they are.

C) Acceptance - unconditional acceptance is imperative to getting people to become prospects. This means that unless people feel like they are accepted they will probably reject your proposals. Acceptance does not mean agreement. It just means that we allow people to be who they are. Through acceptance we can deal with thoughts from potential buyers that may be erroneous.

D) Affection - the way to moving people to being in a position to at least consider what we have to say is to have our entire presentation full of affection for the things we are selling. You cannot expect people to love what you have to offer if you show little or no affection for it. It is vitally important to fill our presentations, words and demeanor with affection for the job we get to do helping people achieve their financial goals.

Persuasion is not control; it is just persuading people to make a good decision that will ultimately bless them and their loved ones.

What Kind of Salesperson Are You?

Many people have entered into the field of sales. But what type of sales person are you?

There are different types of sales people. In this article I will outline the three basic types along with what that will mean to your sales career.

The first one is the person who is in sales taking orders. This person works behind a desk, makes calls or deals with customers who come in. Basically the customer has already expressed an interest in the product and the sales agent's job is to "write the order". They usually do not sell, close or try to persuade someone to do anything.

Most order taker types sales reps are on a salary. Because there is no commission involved for them they are not motivate by money (or the possibility of more of it) and know that whether they close a big sale or a small one, their check remains the same.

My wife worked in a major retailer who had a department and employed these types of salespeople. The sales were mediocre to say the least. When I asked her why the agents were do demotivated, she said there was really no incentive for them to push for more sales. As a result the department never really took off in terms of sales.

The second person presents the products to customers. They walk customers through a presentation and believe the presentation will make the sale. But they fail in understanding that people buy what benefits them. They do not buy because you can deliver a polished presentation.

Sure, they are knowledgeable about their product, confident in their ability to explain it and can answer questions with the best of them. But that's where it ends. I know this person well because this was me. I focused more on being an expert on my product than an expert in selling my product. This belief will not only limit your career but your pocketbook as well.

The third and best salesperson to be in the one who can direct a prospect to make a decision to buy. This is the salesperson that gets paid on a regular basis and earns the money to make sales feel like a career.

They take control. They know from start to finish how this sales cycle works and they guide prospects through the steps. They also are masters at handling objections. They minimize the number of objections they get at the end by answering questions they know the prospect will ask during their presentation.

If you want to see how sales can really provide for you and your family, become a closer today. Take control. Make money!!!

Mastering the Sales Cycle

If you are in sales you have a decision to make; should I stay in sales and make it my career, or should I leave sales and get another job?

If you have decided to stay, will you be just another average agent making an average (or below average) income, or will you strive to excel at your craft?

I believe that if we will pay the price to rise from being just average to above average and look to take this career to another level, then the key is mastering the sales cycle. one you understand how this cycle works you can plan a road trip to success.

Mike Kaplan, author of "Secrets of a Master Closer" had this to say about understanding the sales cycle;

"Before someone will own a product, he must first buy it. Before he will buy it, he has to want it. Before he will want it, he has to be aware of how it will solve his problems. To do that, the prospect has to have his attention directed to the features and benefits of the product that will solve his problem, and he won't let that happen unless he first wants his problem solved - and that won't happen until his problem is found."

I would suggest to anyone serious about selling as a career to learn this paragraph well. It sums up the sales cycle. And when we strive to take detours or go in other directions our sales seem to struggle.

Before you can get to your presentation and discuss features and benefits of our products you have to establish that your prospect wants to go there. I know I have been guilty of meeting people, going right into a presentation and then wondering why it was so hard to close. Here is what I found out;

1) If you don't uncover a problem in your prospect's life, your products won't be viewed as a solution.

2) You must play up the problem in your prospect's life so it is foremost in your conversation. "So you said Mr. Prospect that if something unexpected happened to you, your family would need all the financial assistance they could get. Isn't that right?"

3) You must directly tie the features and benefits of your product to their problem. Forget how great your product is; focus on how it solves their problem and you will have an easier time closing the sale.

Learn the cycle. Master it. Then go out and make a ton of money.

Succeeding in Insurance Sales

There are many books written today on success. It would appear that most of us want to know how to find success in our chosen fields of endeavor.

I want to take this article and discuss how to find success in Insurance sales. I have chosen Insurance as a cornerstone for my own personal income and as such believe that knowing how to make it work is paramount to my future and the security I seek for my family.

What is Insurance Sales? It may seem like a simple answer "sell insurance". But it is much more complicated than that. Many people do not like to be "sold" insurance. When a persons' budget gets tight, insurance is one of the first items to be dropped. It is often categorized as OK to let go of.

Instead of selling people insurance agents need to learn how to listen to what people really need and want. Then, if the situation warrants, show the customer how insurance will get them what they want. For example, if a person is looking to have money to care for their family in the event of their death, insurance is the best vehicle to do that for the least amount of money. We must help people discover how to use insurance to accomplish their financial goals.

Any sales career is motivated by hitting goals and objectives. Insurance is no different. But instead of breaking everything down to just money, try to break it down to productive activity that produces commissions. If you know that you need $1000 a week to live and that your average commission is $500, you need to find out how many presentations do you need to give in order to hit 2 sales a week. You may need 10 presentations a week to hit 2 sales a week. How will you get to 10 presentations a week?

Let me offer two thoughts to get to those 10 presentations a week (or whatever you need to present in order to hit your sales goal);

1) Pursue quality leads - sadly a lot of the leads offered to agents today are garbage. I mean, agents are given cold leads (people who have not expressed an interest in their product) and expected to warm people up to buy. That proves to be a colossal waste of time. Agents who spend 90% of their time prospecting rarely make it in this business. You have to seek out higher quality leads so that the likelihood of closing a sale is great. Referrals are great but you have to position yourself to receive them. Focus your attention on getting the best quality lead you can. That is a lead where

people have expressed an interest in your product at some time and you are talking to someone who is still interested.

2) Improve your closing ratio- the better you are at closing the sale, the quicker you will hit your goal and the more money you will make. In our example we said 10 presentations equal 2 sales. What if you closed 3 sales on 10 presentations? You would make 50% more money and not have seen more people. What if you close 4 sales on 10 presentations? You just doubled your income.

Practicing the things that happened during your closed sales is one of the best ways to improve you closing ratio. Commit to becoming great at your profession. Pay the price to learn what you do well. Become an expert at your job.

And remember, your job is selling; insurance just happens to be your product of choice.

5 Tips to Increase Referrals

There are different types of leads that an Insurance agent can get. I want to categorize them and then begin a discussion on referrals;

1) Cold leads - these leads are to people who have expressed no prior interest in your product and the agent has no prior knowledge that they will have an interest.

2) Warm leads - these leads are to people who may have an interest in your product but more importantly they have a relationship either with the agent or someone the agent knows.

3) Hot leads - these people have expressed an interest in the agent's products and will meet with him to discuss purchasing the product. these are the best leads to have.

Referrals come when someone we have done business with tells someone they know about our products. When we contact them the fact that there is a mutual connection between us allows the agent to give a presentation and possibly make a sale.

Referrals can make our lives so much easier. Not only are they more likely to be warm leads which are met with less resistance for new customers but they are much cheaper to come by than the leads you have to purchase. An agent who does most of his business by referrals will find that his cost to do business will be a lot less than an agent that has to rely on leads.

Here are 5 tips on how to increase your referral business;

A) Always ask for a referral - In every situation, whether you sell your product or not, always ask for a referral. Find out if people know someone who can benefit from what you have to offer.

B) Keep good records of all people you do business with and those you want to do business with - following up on all your contacts will help you to remember to ask for referrals. If a person doesn't become a client they can still be a good referral base.

C) Thank those who give you referrals at least once a year- Remember days that are important to people (birthdays, anniversaries, etc.) and they will remember you.

D) If a referral doesn't purchase a policy from you today, stay in touch; he may tomorrow - never take no to mean never. It just means not now.

E) Commit to building a source for new referrals - referrals are great and the longer you stay in this business, the easier they will make sales for you.

I hope this book has been a help to you. I have tried to cover the various aspects of an Insurance position.

If after reading this you are still ready to get going (or stay with the business) more power to you. If you have questions begin to ask other Insurance professionals.

This is your career. Live it and love it.

Jeff

For additional resources visit the following:

www.amazon.com

www.lordshipinc.com